MADE OF
FLOWERS
AND STEEL

THE 1 VERSE POETRY COLLECTION

SAMEER KOCHURE

Copyright © 2021 by Sameer Kochure.

All rights reserved. No part of this publication may be reproduced, distributed or transmitted in any form or by any means, including photocopying, recording, or other electronic or mechanical methods, without the prior written permission of the publisher, except in the case of brief quotations embodied in critical reviews and certain other noncommercial uses permitted by copyright law. Send permission requests to the address below:

sameer(@)channelinghigherwisdom(.)com

B19, Sangam CHS, Sai Baba Road,

Off SV Road, Santacruz West,

Mumbai - 54, India.

Author photo by Ahsan Ali.

Publisher's Note: This is a work of fiction. Names, characters, places, concepts, and ideas are a product of the author's imagination. Locales and public names are sometimes used for atmospheric purposes. Any resemblance to actual people, living or dead, or to businesses, companies, events, institutions, or locales is completely coincidental.

Written and Published by Sameer Kochure.

Made of Flowers and Steel | Sameer Kochure — First Edition | Print | Paperback

ISBN 9789354937446

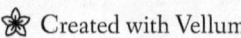 Created with Vellum

PRAISE FOR SAMEER KOCHURE'S BOOKS

A soothing read... it instantly puts a smile on your face! :)

— READER REVIEW

Very cute and same time educating book. I recommend it to everyone... if you had a bad day or a good one.

— READER REVIEW

And all of a sudden, the memory of my loved ones flashed back. The story went straight to my heart.

— READER REVIEW

Very nice collection of stories about big questions of life, presented in a very delightful and easy to consume way. I would definitely give it to my teenager kids to read it as well!

— GOODREADS REVIEW

Sameer has distilled the "WISDOM OF THE MASTERS" in just about 100 pages... It is as if the message is for you as you needed it, at this point of time... Please read this book to evolve spiritually. This book will make you happy.

— READER REVIEW

A light insightful read into every human mind. The book connects to the child in everyone and answers the issues faced by every adult. A must have on every kindle for the days when child like wonder is needed the most.

— READER REVIEW

This was a wonderful spiritual story about the friendship between a young boy and the universe. A story about how to think differently than you might at this time and how to appreciate what is around you. It may answer some of your questions, ease your fears or make you look at life differently, no matter what situations arise.

— GOODREADS REVIEW

CONTENTS

Dear Reader   11

1. The Warrior   13
2. A Love Split in Two   15
3. A Shorter List   17
4. Ladylike   19
5. Roar   20
6. The Whole World   22
7. Trample   25
8. Moments So Rare   27
9. Spending My Love   29
10. Everything Must Go   31
11. Material   33
12. Mould   34
13. What Came After   36
14. Divine Math   41
15. Insightful Observations   43
16. Okay Love   45
17. A Good Hiding Spot   46
18. Lonely Streets   47
19. Mushroom Top   49
20. A Fair Trade   52
21. The Team of Me   53
22. The Ying in the Yang   55
23. The Best   57
24. Whole and Complete   58
25. War Paint   60
26. The Same Soul   61

27. The Blue Bowl — 62
28. Goodbye — 65
29. Ambush — 66
30. A Clever Trick — 67
31. Not a Bargain — 69
32. Unfiltered Discontent — 70
33. The Fun Me — 73
34. The One — 74
35. Tiger Stripes — 76
36. You being You — 77
37. Use Abuse — 79
38. Leave — 80
39. Your Body Loves You — 81
40. Nowhere — 85
41. Signals — 86
42. Slur — 88
43. The Three Witnesses — 89
44. True — 92
45. A Rich Husband — 93
46. Control — 95
47. God on Earth — 100
48. Sisterhood — 101
49. How Lucky — 105
50. Enjoy the Game — 106
51. How to Beat a Woman — 108
52. Who You Are — 110
53. Stalker — 111
54. Take a Stand — 116
55. A Rare Treasure — 117
56. Birds and Bees — 118
57. The Locksmith — 120
58. No. — 123
59. Make Belief — 126

60. Hope	127
61. Cycle of Hurt	129
62. Torn	131
63. Loss	132
64. An Eternal Earth	133
65. Fresh as Flowers	136
66. Robbed	138
67. The Sun and the Stars	140
68. Behind Closed Doors	143
69. Just Saying	145
70. Love at First Flight	146
71. No Rush	148
72. The Eternal Kind	149
73. A Whole Lot of Love	151
74. The Shield	153
75. Radiance	155
76. Courage	157
77. Moving in	159
78. A Dancing Soul	162
79. A Happy Puppy	163
80. Strength of Character	165
81. Timeless	166
82. Home	168
83. My Happy Place	170
84. The Fears I Feel	172
85. The War Within	176
86. Work in Progress	178
87. The Silent Witness	179
88. Uniqueness	182
89. Your Blank Page	184
90. Ever After	187
91. We Got This	189
92. Tags	190

93. Content	192
94. Seen and Heard	194
95. Guarded	196
96. A Chance Encounter	198
97. Conquer	201
98. The Deal	202
99. Family	204
100. Tinpot	206
101. Here On	209
An Unimportant Thing	214
Big Plans	216
A Cloudy Day	218
All Right	221
Acknowledgments	223
A Gift With Your Name On It	227
Also by Sameer Kochure	229
Your Short Story	231
About the Author	233
Care Section	235
Buy or Borrow	241
Gratitude	243

to Aai, my mom,
Sunanda Pramod Kochure,
the light of my universe,
the one made of the sweetest flowers,
and the kindest steel.

DEAR READER

From times long forgotten, poets around the world have sung praises about the physical beauty of women.

Few have recognised their mettle.

The inherent power that exists in all women. Forget poets and lovers, women themselves often fail to recognise their own inner strength and tenacity.

Sometimes, that power needs to be invoked.

That's my intention with this book. To honour the raw grit and the sublime strength that hides behind the beauty. And, if need be, to give it a good shake and wake it up.

By the time you are done reading, you'll have a newfound love and respect for yourself and for all the women in your life.

That's a promise I intend to keep.

Love,
> Sameer Kochure.
> 19th July 2021.

THE WARRIOR

she steps out in the cold
while her child, her world,
sleeps warm in the bed inside
she locks the door
and crosses the street in the dark
the dogs haven't stirred yet
and the clouds are yet to greet the sun
she catches her bus
and tries to nap on the way
how does she do this every single day?
it seems, she loves to travel
only in the dark...
for by the time she returns,
the outside will be bathed
in the same shade of blue

and when she steps into her home,
her child will almost be ready for bed again
his smile though, like always,
will take away all the aches
of her another working day.

        she looks like she's made of flowers
            but she's really made of steel.

2

A LOVE SPLIT IN TWO

it is impossible
for two women to share
the love of one man
yet, i know i can make it work
only because i love my man
and he loves us both,
equally and differently.
however different
the two most important women
in his life may be from one another
we at least have one thing in common,
he won't be able to give one up
for the sake of the other.
so... i won't make him choose
i would rather make a new friend

someone riper and wiser
and who knows, some day, like him,
i may even learn to call her 'mom'
and mean it too.
now, no one is keeping score
but i know, when he sees me try,
my man will smile a little more.

        i am made of flowers
        i am made of steel.

3

A SHORTER LIST

thank you dear stranger
for raping me with your eyes
would you be kind enough
to leave your name as well please?
so when, years later,
the love of my life questions me
on my trust issues,
i can give me him
a long list of reasons,
and i wouldn't want to miss
your valuable contribution...
don't worry, i am strong enough,
i will soon learn to cope
someday though, it may be

your daughter in my heels...
with a much shorter list, i hope.

    for we are all made of flowers,
        just as we are made of steel.

4

LADYLIKE

i deadlift
and i drive a truck
if you have a problem with that,
if you think it isn't very 'ladylike'
i invite you to step into my lane
and voice your objections
stand a little to the left please
right there, perfect.
now hold still while i rev and
the rubber gets ready to burn.

      i may be made of flowers
      but i am 100% made of steel.

5

ROAR

turns out
all girls are born with vocal cords.
the entire speech apparatus
in their tiny throats
shapes up just as fast and slow
as does the one in the boys' throats
should someone
keep track of the noise levels,
they'll find that
the cries and wails of both
are of almost equal volume too
and then something strange happens
the girls grow up.
the society, the customs,
the rituals, the etiquettes,

the restrictions, the prejudices,
all of them kick in
and somewhere between
being born and being brought up
that voice starts fading
by the time
the butterfly finds its wings
often, only a whimper remains
it takes courage
to find that voice once again
and it takes
someone, or something,
to believe in you
to, once again,
bring out that roar in you.
for you, let that someone be me
and let that something be these words.

> for you are made of flowers
> you are made of steel.

6

THE WHOLE WORLD

the metallurgist said
'metals and minerals,
that's what makes our world'
the chemist told me
it's all in the composition...
it's all one big chemical cocktail,
i can give you
the formula for the whole world,
if you have but a moment...
the religious man told me
the world is god's abode,
and god is one
the teacher told me
the world is a floating orb,
going around in circles,

for measurable millenniums...
the businessman told me
the world is real estate...
some he owns,
the rest he wishes he owned
the artist told me
the world is a masterpiece
he will paint someday
the new-age vlogger told me
the world is energy manifested
by our collective spirits...
then, i asked you, my child,
what is the world
and you looked at me and said,
'*...you, momma?*'
oh, how i melted at that...
but you are wrong my dear
i am not your world
but you are mine.

      i am made of flowers
      i am made of steel,
and of all the things i am, and will ever be,
   being your *momma* is a real treat.

7

TRAMPLE

it's one thing
to admire a flower from afar
to quietly and respectfully
appreciate its beauty
as one of the ultimate's finest creations
or to admire the sheer brilliance
of nature at work within it...
and it's another thing to manhandle it,
crush it or pluck it
without permission
...
the beauty of the flower is its gift
not a crime to be punished
the hand that crushes it may, sadly,
get away with a flower or two

but that hand
is sure to encounter a thorn
that will drain
all its blood of well-earned scorn

                        we are made of flowers,
                        but don't you dare forget,
                        we are also made of steel.

MOMENTS SO RARE

she's the master of small talk
she's good at making friends
she knows how to impress
at any interview
and charm even the quiet ones
at a house party
she can talk her way
out of pretty much anything...
and that's why
she loves the man,
and the moments,
that leave her
wonderfully speechless

she's made of flowers
she's made of steel.

SPENDING MY LOVE

i spent a lot of my life
waiting for love to show up
and it never did...
then i grew tired of waiting
and started spending my love
on the ones hungry for it instead.
i didn't even realise
exactly when
the love i so freely gave away
slipped right back into my life,
pitched a tent and made home.

        i am made of flowers
        i am made of steel

and i auto-magically receive,
the more i give.

10

EVERYTHING MUST GO

'you can't wear that'
'that's too bold'
'that's too small'
'too revealing'
'so last season'
'you can't be serious'
'oh you can't carry that off, dear'
'try a bigger size'
...
it's like opinions were
on a clearance sale
and all were screaming
take me home...
take me home...
we belong together

make me yours...

...

sorry opinions
i ain't that easy
my standards are high
and none of you stand a chance.

    i look like i am made of flowers
    but i am really made of steel.

MATERIAL

melts at the sight of babies
and anyone in distress…
hardens in the face of discrimination
and danger to her loved ones
her heart is made of mysterious materials…
the ones, as yet, unknown to man
that's why a man finds it so hard to win it over
for this material will never trust itself
to the care of an unworthy man.

        she's made of flowers,
        just as she's made of steel.

12

MOULD

it's kinda funny really
how every generation
modifies and makes
their own version
of a nice little mould
the one stamped with -
cute, subservient and mute...
and then expects us women
to conform to that mould.
and when we don't, well,
every generation has
their own favourite names for it
witch, trouble, easy, sl-
you've heard them all before
wonder if they'll ever learn

MADE OF FLOWERS AND STEEL

the moulds won't fit anymore
for the ones shaping us now,
is no one else, but us.

    we are made of flowers
    and we forge ourselves in steel.

WHAT CAME AFTER

never thought
there may be something
more horrible than being raped
until it happened to me...
rape is bad enough
but it hurts so much more
when your rapist is the one
you called your boyfriend
until that incident...
and if that wasn't painful enough,
the ones meant
to serve and protect - the cops,
they told me that
the juries almost never convict
a rapist who was also

an intimate friend...
i used to think
getting raped must be horrible
then i discovered
something so much worse...
i chose to fight.
to allow myself
to get humiliated in court,
you know,
because even the accused,
and his attorney,
is given a fair chance at defence,
that's the hallmark
of a developed society
innocent until proven guilty.
anyway, the cops were right all along
he walked.
all over the broken pieces of myself
which i decided to pick up...
every last one.
there were times when somehow,
the rape itself felt like
the least horrible
of the things that followed.
and so, i vowed.
if i can save one girl from this,

my nightmare
would serve a higher purpose.
so i made weapons of my words
and started sharing my story
so that my sisters -
all the girls in the world,
never face this situation,
or at least they handle it
so much better.
i tell my tale so that we women
become better cops, lawyers and juries.
so we learn how to compassionately
sit down with our lovers,
and the ones
who hold our trust,
and educate them
on the difference
between love and violence.
to help them develop their egos
to be so strong
that our 'no'
does not make them feel
diminished in any way
the ones who hurt other people
are hurting inside too...
so as a part of society,

MADE OF FLOWERS AND STEEL

it's also up to us women
to raise better men
that's the goal
i have set myself,
to build an army
of women so strong,
they can protect and
defend themselves
against any evil.
and an army of women
so compassionate that
they transform evil
into love and respect.
that's my mission
won't you join me on it, sister?

    because you may be made of flowers
    but never forget, you are also made of steel.

DIVINE MATH

i said thank you
for the one thing that was
right in my life,
and suddenly,
there were two...
i felt grateful for them both,
and then, there were more...
and that's how i learnt
this universe's equation,
and cracked its divine math...
the way to enjoy more blessings
is to count the ones i already have.
so, here are two more,

i am made of flowers
i am made of steel,
and when i take an honest look at my life,
i am so blessed indeed.

15

INSIGHTFUL OBSERVATIONS

thanks dear almost stranger,
my so called 'fan'
and 'follower'
from the inter-webs
thank you so much
for your
insightful observations
on my holiday weight gain...
wish you were
a bit more like me though,
and couldn't care less
for flowers come in
all shapes and sizes,
and the heavier it is,
the stronger

is steel known to be.

> i am made of flowers,
> i am made of steel
> and I only choose to hear
> the words that heal.

OKAY LOVE

when your heart's left
bleeding on the floor
by their actions, absence or words
pick it up gently and whisper to it -

>you'll be okay, my love,
>you are made of flowers and steel.

A GOOD HIDING SPOT

darkness is smart
it knows all the blind spots
that's why, sometimes,
it hides right behind
the brightest source of light
...
and that's why,
my trust isn't easily given
it must be hard earned.

>for i am made of flowers
>i am made of steel,
>and i am so worth the time you invest
>to deserve my keep.

LONELY STREETS

in this universe so full of sunshine
what kind of world have we built
that a woman must step with caution
for the fear of darkness lurking
around every lonely street corner?
it's easy to attribute the darkness
to a small group of the species,
the powerless men who feign power...
but it's also up to the light,
us women, to be strong and capable
so much so that darkness grows terrified
of crossing us in any street.

        for we are made of flowers

and when pushed into a corner,
we will cut you like steel.

MUSHROOM TOP

i once thought,
i will make my home
on a mushroom top...
i'll choose a nice plump one
all colourful, strong and pretty...
and whenever it will rain
i'll step under its umbrella again
have a little bonfire,
sing some songs and
roast white marshmallows
till they looked like cocoa...
and when it was warm and sunny
i'll drag out the hammock
right on to its roof,
lay down with a nice book...

the rope ladder for my friends
would always be down,
and the front door
for them, forever open...
back then, my needs and wants
were quite simple
nature was my slice of heaven
and the nameplate
outside my little door
correctly declared
'happiness lives here'
i've grown a bit since
but deep down,
i'm still the same...
always keeping an eye out
for some mushroom real estate.

    i'm made of flowers
    i'm made of steel
    and i am such a child
    deep underneath.

MADE OF FLOWERS AND STEEL

A FAIR TRADE

i was born with love
the world traded it for hate
before i turned eight...
now i am older and wiser
so i give my love freely to all
i just don't expect a fair trade.

> i am made of flowers
> i am made of steel
> i know life isn't fair,
> so i don't expect love to be.

THE TEAM OF ME

i am on the team of me
i am my biggest fan
i slap my back and tell me
it's gonna be okay
when it feels like
it will never be
i cheer myself up
when i am feeling down
i give me a pep talk
i give me a ted talk
i am the one who really listens
when i need to talk
i am the one
who pampers me and
takes me shopping,

when life has been
too hard too long
i am the shoulder i lean on
i am the one
who gives me strength
after a break up...
i am my favourite summer song
i have dear friends,
soul sisters too,
but above them all,
the truest best friend
to me, is me.

      i am made of flowers
      i am made of steel
how can i expect anyone to be on my team,
    if i won't be on the team of me?

THE YING IN THE YANG

there are those who claim
god is a woman
i don't have an opinion
on the matter
but i would like to observe
that nature has given
the bulk of the responsibility
of creation to the feminine
of almost all species.
the masculine
is indispensable, of course.
the ying in the yang
the zig in the zag
a part that's vital to the whole
but let's be honest,

where would the world be
if it weren't for us women
keeping it decent and
holding it up?

>for we are made of flowers,
>we are made of steel.

THE BEST

the best that i can do for you
is to be the best me i can ever be.

        i am made of flowers
        i am made of steel.

WHOLE AND COMPLETE

that's a real possibility
she knows it
she used to fear it once
now she puts on a brave face
reassures her gang,
and her mum,
that she doesn't need anyone to be happy
she's whole and complete by herself...
still
somewhere deep inside, the doubts remain
what if i am wrong?
what if i should have settled for less?
there were plenty of opportunities,
maybe i made a mistake?
what if i have to do this all by myself?

...

the doubts never go away
but she gets stronger by the day.

    she thinks she's made of flowers
      but she's really made of steel.

WAR PAINT

you look at me and see a princess
that's the magic of my makeup
for it is not really makeup
nor am i really a princess
the makeup is my war paint
and my pretty clothes
are my armour in disguise
treat me as a princess though
and that's what you'll get.
but if you treat me bad
you better prepare from my wrath.

      i look like flowers,
          but i am hardened steel.

THE SAME SOUL

most days
i love animals
way more than
i love humans
some rare days in between
i love them both equal.

    i'm made of flowers
    i'm made of steel
    and i know that all living beings
    share the same soul underneath.

THE BLUE BOWL

i still hear those words, dad
just the way you said them...
i even remember the way you looked
that beautiful summer day...
funny how memories work, right?
i don't remember what
i had for breakfast this morning
but i hear those words from 21 years ago
just as i heard them for the first time
as i stood at the sink
looking at the broken bowl
that had slipped through
my tiny soapy fingers...
you didn't even sound angry
as you said,

'you really can't
do anything, can you?'
i remember the rainbow lights
dancing in the foam becoming brighter
by the tears in my eyes.
i am sure you forgot all about
that bowl before the day,
or the week was out
while i came to know
that blue bowl intimately
as it stayed with me for 2 decades...
long it used to cut and stab me
especially when it was time for me
to do something new...
first job, first kiss, first labour...
that bowl, and those words
would come and find me, right on cue
filling me with doubt
'how can i do this
if i can't do anything?'
it took a whole lot of self love,
caring and nurturing by kind
and loving souls to win me back
my lost confidence
in time, i learnt to bury
that blue bowl and let go of it

but the words remain.
they still mock me
whenever they feel like...
hoping to catch me by surprise.
but now, i have a fitting answer for them.
whenever they ask
'you really can't do anything, can you?'
i just smile and say, 'watch me.'

    i look like i am made of flowers,
        but i am so made of steel.

GOODBYE

you wonder why did i leave...
don't you remember
how you used to hug me tight?
it would have been nice,
your grip was warm and strong...
but your doubts were stronger.
and in your arms
i could hardly breathe.

> i am made of flowers,
> i am made of steel
> and i respect me enough to know
> when to stay and when to leave.

AMBUSH

when anxiety ambushes you
and gives you a chill....
look it in the eye,
give it your sweet smile
and say,

'you can't get me silly....
don't you know,
i am made of flowers and steel?'

A CLEVER TRICK

there is no biological reason
for you to look like me
so how do i see
so much of me in you?
yes, there is absolutely
no denying it
you are mine alright
my flesh and blood
my hopes and dreams
my prayers and blessings
it was another one
of your clever tricks
to try and fool me by
choosing another womb...
well, you got me...

come now,
finish your greens.

        i'm made of flowers,
        i'm made of steel
        and you, my dear,
        are made of me.

NOT A BARGAIN

don't be a bargain
be worth it.
you already are,
you just need to act
like you know it too.

>for you are made of flowers,
>you are made of steel.

UNFILTERED DISCONTENT

i was once
scrolling through on my phone
in the dark, late at night,
fighting sleep, when i realised
the social feed kept feeding me
unfiltered discontent
...discontent about who i am,
what i look like, and
where i have reached so far in my life
...it kept whispering in my ears
'you are not good enough'
...
that's when i figured out
how their algorithms work
they don't want to entertain

or engage me,
they want to entrap me...
'feeling not good enough? here, buy this.'
stream some porn, buy a new dress,
how about a protein shake,
shhh... don't tell anyone,
here's a get rich quick secret,
how to know he's cheating on you,
how to make her scream in the bedroom...
sheesh...
that's when i realised
how social media sees us
and wants us to feel...
like a mess and a total failure...
so they can sell us the way out of it,
how nice.
well,
i am not buying anymore.
i came here for friends,
and met a lot of brands instead
someone selling products,
someone selling themselves
hawking their ideas, opinions and fears...
i ain't in the market for that anymore.
i want real friends, real connections
that lift me up, not bring me down

i know it won't be easy
thanks to the years
of scrolling up and swiping right
but i know if anyone can do it,
i know it is me, i believe in me.
so, here's me tucking in and logging off
and no, i don't need you to like,
subscribe and comment on my update.
i'll see you out in the real world,
well rested after a good night's sleep.

        i am made of flowers,
        i am made of steel
and right now, i am logging off
        and going to sleep.

THE FUN ME

i'm me
most of the times...
but when i'm the most fun me
that's usually because
i'm with the ones
that just let me be.

        i'm made of flowers,
         i'm made of steel.

THE ONE

i'm both,
more than a single digit,
and less than it
at the same time.
not sure what you were expecting
but that is how it is.
i'm strong and capable though
even malleable like pure gold,
so with a little bit of your
love and support,
i can lose some and gain some,
a bit of both, as needed,
to make a complete whole.
the full, final and the ultimate...
one.

the one for you.
of course, only if you
would do the same for me,
that goes both ways too.

> i'm made of flowers
> i'm made of steel,
> so tell me,
> are you the one for me?

TIGER STRIPES

those are not stretch marks
those are my tiger stripes...
my body, like my spirit,
was born to be untamed and wild.

>i am made of exotic wild flowers
>and i have claws of steel.

YOU BEING YOU

the sun knows no night...
it never gets to meet
the stars in the dark sky...
and it never knows the beauty
it inspires throughout the universe.
the sun does all this
just by being true to itself,
and sharing its light.
and that's why
you need to keep shining
your own light.
for you never know
which corner of the universe
is lit up bright

and made more beautiful
by you being you.

    for you are made of flowers
      you are made of steel.

USE ABUSE

when someone
wants to use you,
or treats you
like a piece of meat,
remind yourself

> you are made of
> flowers and steel.

LEAVE

when they
slam the door
and leave you
all alone
crying on the floor,
hold your own hand
and tell yourself
it will take a little time,
but i'll heal just fine.

      for i am made of flowers
        i am made of steel.

39

YOUR BODY LOVES YOU

the human body is designed
to function at peak levels
without causing damage to itself.
various safety and task optimising functions
kick in automatically when required.
the easiest example
to understand this phenomenon
is to think of how your pupils dilate
to protect themselves
and give you a better vision
in different lighting conditions.
a far more difficult phenomenon
to understand is the female body's response
to any form of vaginal penetration
- producing natural lubrication.

the body produces this response
to prevent unnecessary injury
and discomfort to the body itself.
so when a woman's vagina gets wet
while she's being raped,
it is not because she's enjoying it.
it is because the body's automatic response
to any form of penetration,
consensual or not, has kicked in.
it's not desire, it's a biological response.
unfortunately, not enough victims
know this and go on blaming themselves
for mistaking their body's natural response
as getting aroused during a rape.
they get confused and wonder
whether they were subconsciously enjoying it.
they find that thought itself revolting.
they sometimes start buying into
the society's horrible remarks
'she must've been asking for it'

...

no, you were not aroused.
yes, it is still a rape.
this may not be much of a poem,
but if it didn't have
your conscious permission,

it was very much a rape.
you were the victim.
do not torture yourself over
your body's self protection response.
you are not to be blamed.
your body did what it did
because it loves you and
wants to keep you safe.
it's time for you to show
some of that love to yourself as well.

>   for the world may sometimes
>   treat you cold as steel,
>   but don't you forget, my child,
>   you are made of flowers so sweet.

NOWHERE

when love
is running low
and there's
nowhere left to go
know that you are
stronger than before.

        for you are
        made of flowers and steel.

SIGNALS

so i went shopping the other day
it's easy for me usually, enjoyable even,
but this time it was impossible...
i was looking for something
that wasn't 'asking for it'...
i did some research when you,
my partner, my confidant,
told me the reason
i almost got kidnapped
and possibly assaulted,
was because my clothing
was sending out the wrong message...
so i researched, like i did my uni thesis.
turns out jeans, overalls, ill-fitting clothes,
rags of the homeless...

basically anything we women wear,
all of them fall under
the 'asking for it' category...
for a moment i considered
being a nudist hippy
if they still exist...
then i realised
i don't need to change my clothing...
i just need to change the people
i was turning to for love and support.
so this is where 'us' ends.
why do you look so surprised?
i thought you were an expert at reading
the 'asking for it' signals.

    i'm made of flowers
    and i'm so made of steel.

SLUR

when they use a slur
leave them in a blur.
know your own worth.

    'cos you, my dear, are
    made of flowers and steel.

THE THREE WITNESSES

she said you'll never win
it'll come down
to your word or mine
i am a respected member
of the society,
hold an important
and a prestigious job,
move in the right circles,
while you stock the aisles
where my servants shop.
it's only wise to forget
this ever happened
and move on with your life.
i told her she need not worry
i didn't meant to cause a ruckus

not because i'm powerless,
but because i know that
justice will be served
where it is rightly due
and i'll be rewarded
for my troubles
from means as yet unknown.
i wouldn't cause a scene
not for the reasons she listed
or her position...
i felt no need to prove her guilt
because what she did
had 3 infallible witnesses.
me, her and the one above.
she can defend herself well
in the court of law
but how would she ever
prove her innocence
to these 3 silent witnesses?
sometimes my power is tested
when i stand up
and fight for my right
and sometimes
my power is tested
by my capacity to let go.
i am capable of both, and

i choose my battles wisely.

> i am made of flowers
> i am made of steel.
> sometimes i fight and
> sometimes i forgive.

44

TRUE

words are sweet
but actions are true
stay where both value you.

                for you are
            made of flowers and steel.

A RICH HUSBAND

so an interesting thing
happened today.
i was passing
a group of women
in a café earlier in the day...
as i crossed their table
i heard something
that must have started
as a compliment...
perhaps they liked
what i wore,
my clothes or jewellery,
i don't know...
the words i could catch, or rather,
i was meant to catch, were,

'...she must have a rich husband.'
well, i am glad that they liked
what i wore, my shoes or shades,
or whatever else i don't know...
they got one thing right though,
there was a time when
i couldn't afford these things.
i am so grateful i can now.
and no, i do not have a rich husband,
i have a rich me.

    i am made of flowers
    i am made of steel
    and the things they envied,
    i bought them for me.

CONTROL

pockets.
it's almost impossible to find
a piece of clothing
for men without them
and just as difficult finding
women's clothing with them
even most of our business suits
come without pockets.
they fit better,
flow on you nicer - they tell us.
the truth is, even though
we have been
proving ourselves as equal,
if not superior at work,
the society still doesn't want us

to handle our money
nor learn how to manage it well.
it wants us women
to allow the men to be in charge
of our money,
and therefore, our futures.
of course, no designer
is consciously doing this
all of this conditioning is subliminal.
it's planted in our heads
over thousands of generations
for what good are pockets
if a woman must always be home?
everything she needs
is at an arm's distance
in the kitchen or
the bedroom, right?
- now that hidden subtext
makes my blood boil.
that's why i think
it is time for us women
to sew some pockets
on our psyche.
to learn the spiritual
and the practical tools
of making a lot of money

- for it takes both to be wealthy.
it's time for us women
to learn to manage
our money well, on our own.
to learn to multiply it, on our own.
to learn how to
secure our future - on our own.
let's face it,
when we stepped out of our homes
and showed up at work,
work became better.
not just for us, even for the men.
there are numerous studies that show
the morale and productivity improves
when both sexes
work together as equals.
so it will be with money too.
when men and women,
both learn to manage and
multiply it together,
both will be the richer for it.
and's that's the dream
anyone chasing money
aspires to, right?
true wealth and freedom.
that dream begins with

us women stepping up and
taking control of our abundance.
and to be fair,
we have some catching up to do.
making and managing
a lot of money
is a skill some of us
still need to learn and master.
so we may have to study it a bit
read a couple of books,
take an online course or two,
and maybe attend
a few seminars too...
yes, it sounds like work,
and initially it sounds a little scary
intimidating and unfamiliar even,
but never forget,
we have each other
to support us on this journey.
all of our past track record
is proof enough
that we can do anything
we set our mind to.
we can do it just as well as anyone
often, we do it much, much better.
so, let's get new pockets tailored

MADE OF FLOWERS AND STEEL

in on our clothes
and let's be sure
to have them made deep.
let's master this skill too
take control of our finances,
create our future
and build our own fortunes.

    we are made of flowers,
    we are made of steel
    and we won't stop until we've hit gold
    and built our fortunes.

GOD ON EARTH

why does
no one ever tell us
we never get old enough
to not need our mother?

    mom, you were made of flowers
    and you were made of the loveliest steel.

SISTERHOOD

there is much talk
of cyber bullying
but i feel
we don't talk enough
of cyber buddying
yeah, that's a word now
because i just made it up.
it's a phenomenon
that can be observed
when a scared little girl
or a woman of any age really,
in some part of the world
posts some question
on some women's reddit sub
or some such anon forum

and asks something
that she can't ask anyone else
maybe about missing a period
or about the abuse she faces at home
or about the inappropriate advances
she's trying to avoid at work
or about her upcoming interview
after a long stay at home *mumming* spell
or about coping with the frustration
when all attempts at trying to conceive fail
or about the conflicting emotions postpartum...
the questions are as varied
as all our lives are
but there is one thing
in common with such posts -
the woman asking
is being vulnerable
and has turned to strangers
cos there is no one else
in her world who is either
someone reliable or
someone who'll understand or
someone who won't judge.
and when a post like that
hits our newsfeeds
we women do what we do best

we offer love
we offer support
we offer information
we offer a shoulder to cry on
we offer 100 solutions
we offer 1000 suggestions...
and that little girl or woman,
she doesn't feel all alone anymore.
she never was.
you never are.
womanhood is a sisterhood
you are born into.
i don't know you,
perhaps i never will.
the unique paths
that our beautiful lives are on
have brought us together
on this page, on this post,
for this one brief moment.
our paths may diverge right after
and may never
cross again in this lifetime,
but while they intersect,
at this brief point in time,
if i can lift you up, i will.
if i can help you out, i will.

if i can tell you,
it's going to be alright, i will.
this is what i believe
it means to be a woman.
to be there for each other.
i may not be
in your exact situation,
but i'll be your friend,
because,
in another time,
in another place,
i have been in your heels.

    we are made of flowers
    we are made of steel.
    and we got each other's back
    when in need.

HOW LUCKY

sure,
it's nice to have someone.
but you don't need someone
you got you.
and, my oh my,
how lucky of you.

> you are made of flowers
> you are made of steel.

50

ENJOY THE GAME

so you want to finish on my face
and you want me to be okay with it?
full points to you
on the courage department
it may not have been easy to ask,
at least i hope it wasn't...
anyway, since it is a matter of courage
let me show you some as well,
"no, it's not okay."
let's make love, not shoot porn
let's experiment, let's play
in a way both of us can enjoy the game.
none of us need feel dirty and
used like a rag after.
let's explore, and find ways

to make it a spiritual experience even...
something that helps us
rise higher in conscience
that's what i am always in the mood for...

>	for i am made of flowers,
>		i am made of steel.

HOW TO BEAT A WOMAN

here's a handy little guide
on when and how to beat a woman
beat her at waking up early
beat her at excelling
at career and at home
beat her at making the kids
ready for school
beat her at planning anniversaries
beat her to getting a master's degree
while raising two kids
beat her at hosting dinners
for your extended family
beat her to managing
your home finances like a pro
beat her at stepping up and

being the sole breadwinner,
if required
beat her at being socially confident
beat her at showing affection
beat her at multitasking
beat her to making friends
with neighbours
beat her at being best friends
with your children
beat her at making her partner
feel like a million bucks
beat her at giving neck rubs
beat her at kissing the pain away
beat her at being responsible...
...
beat us women where it really matters.

        for we are made of flowers,
        and we are made of steel.

52

WHO YOU ARE

diamonds and pearls
empires and kingdoms
pale in comparison
to the treasure that you are.

    you are made of flowers
    you are made of steel
it's okay to doubt it once in a while, but
know that you are so precious indeed.

STALKER

i've a stalker
we've been at it for a while now
he's no longer a stranger
i know he's committed
and always around
so i'm careful
and watch my step...
still, ever so often
he catches me unaware
sometimes when
i'm trying to sleep at night
sometimes when
i feel how much
i'm lagging behind in life
sometimes while i'm lost

in endless scroll on my phone
sometimes when
i'm by myself at home
he sneaks up on me
and sucks out
all the light in the room
he goes by the tag of depression
and his job is oppression...
to call a thing
by its true name
is to begin to understand it.
depression is the facade,
its true name is destruction.
depression makes it
sound like a condition
but it is an untamed force that,
if left unchecked and unleashed,
destroys everything in its path...
i learnt it the hard way
but i learnt my lesson fast
instead of digging myself
further into the hole
i focused on building a ladder
to bring me out of it
a book, a song, a video,
a supportive online forum,

sensible offline friends,
stories of the ones
who were on the same journey
and who made it out okay,
i gathered them all
and built them into steps
for my stepladder.
little by little
i kept fighting the good fight
it a was long, hard climb
and like all the worthy, uphill hikes,
i broke free and reached the summit
right beyond my breaking point.
up here, just a few steps and
a few miles away from my stalker,
there was bright sunshine
and happy times...
they were always here,
waiting for me to show up.
...
i'm sharing my story
so you have something to start with
in case you are in need of timber
for your own ladder...
i know sometimes
one can find themselves

surrounded by
so much darkness
that there is
no hint of light.
but please know that
the light exists
a way out exists
i found it, and
here i am, holding out my hand
to help you find it too...
let's stop digging this hole
and start working on your ladder now
there is a way out
and the only one
who can walk it for you, is you.
every step counts
so keep on keeping on
be kind and be gentle
on yourself along the way
makes no sense
to make it harder
than it has to be
just one step forward
just one step upward
just one step at a time
that's all it takes,

so keep at it please
and when you make it to the top,
you will find me waiting for you
with a warm cup and a warm hug,
saving you a spot in the sun.

> for you are made of flowers
> you are made of steel
> and your beautiful life, my dear,
> is meant to be lived.

TAKE A STAND

when
the whole world
stands against you,
be the one who
stands strong
and stands firm
for you.

> for you are made of flowers
> you are made of steel.

A RARE TREASURE

keep your heart
under a lock and key.
better still,
throw away the key.
the one who takes
the effort to
find it in the abyss
will have
proved his worth.

    for you are made of flowers
    you are made of steel,
    and you may or may not know it,
    but you are a treasure indeed.

56

BIRDS AND BEES

i was born 34 years ago
and got strong enough
to come out 5 years ago.
once free, i thought,
now i would like to know
where to go
to claim back
my 29 un-lived years?
will someone please tell me,
who owes them to me?
is it the world?
the society?
my parents?
the altar?
or myself -

for being afraid
and unsure?
then i realised
i was still
trapped in that hell
if i was looking back at it.
looking for answers
that may never exist.
so now, i look forward
and live my life so well...
after all, i have 29 years
to make up for and
to really, simply, freely live.

       i am made of flowers
       i am made of steel
       and i am finally free,
       just like the birds and the bees.

THE LOCKSMITH

the locksmith was puzzled
he was a man, he wouldn't understand.
'just to be sure,' he asked,
'you want me to
install this lock... on this door?'
i nodded.
he said, 'but this is a strong
and an expensive lock...
people always ask me
to install it on their main doors...
you know to keep the dangers out...'
i said, 'and that's why,
i want it on my bedroom door.
the danger pounding drunkenly
late night at my door

doesn't come from outside.'
his face told me
he finally understood.
he asked,
'what else could i do to help?'
well, well.
you just did, i thought.
you just helped me
consider the cliché
maybe, it's not all men after all.
i found myself saying,
'i am helping myself
with this lock already.
but it's an experiment really.
tell you what, just save my number.'
he nodded, 'sure thing,
think of me as your big brother,
call me anytime, day or night,
whenever you need help, okay?'
i was touched by this kindness
from someone who was
a total stranger but a moment ago.
not. all. men. indeed.
i said, 'thank you.
i can take care of myself.
the reason i want you

to save my number
is if my experiment doesn't work,
i'm calling you next week
to come in and change the keys
on my front door.'
he smiled, relieved
to hear the steel in my voice.
he could see that
i was in a bad situation,
but i was far from weak.

    i am made of flowers
    i am made of steel... and i got this.

58

NO.

think of a driving license
and think of a job.
a driving license gives you
full freedom to drive
pretty much
as long as you want
...unless you screw up
big time and
get it cancelled.
a job on the other hand
can be taken away from you
at any time.
valid reason or not,
with or without your fault.
and if you've ever been fired before,

you know that
there is nothing you can do
to reverse that decision...
being fired is being fired.
the best thing to do
is to just accept it,
hold your head high
and walk away
with your dignity intact.
it's just a job,
you'll soon have another one,
more likely, a nicer one.
and that's exactly
how consent works.
not like a driving license
more like a job.
it can be taken away any time
valid reason or not,
with or without your fault.
just respect it please,
don't make it weird.
consent is not consent
unless it can be taken away.
we may or may not share the reason
but trust us, we have a good one.
just hold your head high

and walk away.
you'll earn more of our respect that way
and tomorrow will be a new day.

> we are made of flowers
> we are made of steel
> and just like you,
> we are blessed with free will.

MAKE BELIEF

i must be a child at heart
for i still believe
in miracles and et al
for how else do i explain
what it means to me
to have found you and
to get to spend my life
simply loving you...

    i am made of flowers
    i am made of steel,
i used to think fairy tales were just tales
    until they came true for me.

HOPE

every day
it rises with dawn
i've been patient
i've been strong
been through
many such days...
longer than
i could've imagined
going on...
day after day...
days have come and
days have gone.
and here i am
at the end of today,
still waiting

still praying
still hanging on.
maybe tomorrow then?
yes tomorrow.
let tomorrow
be the day
when...
...

        i am made of flowers
         i am made of steel
    and in me, hope still lives.

CYCLE OF HURT

push pins
paper shredder
pencil sharpener
sharpened pencils
stapler
paper clips
plastic forks
takeout knifes
finger slamming drawers
white board duster...
pantry cabinet that could
accidentally open in my face...
...
there were times
i would make mental notes at work,

count the number of things
that could hurt...
i was just continuing
the process you started
it was our little cycle of torture
first you to me
then me to me...
ironically it was a friend at work
who read the signs,
she had been there before
she had overcome it before.
thanks to her support
i now count you in my past
and every morning at work
i count the flowers
in the receptionist's vase.

    i am made of flowers
    i am made of steel
and that friend of mine from work,
    she's made of all things sweet.

TORN

when the world
tries to tear you down,
do it brick by brick,
do it slowly if you will,
but build yourself
right back up.

>for you are made of flowers
>you are made of steel.

LOSS

i never get to say
i love you again
and you never get to say
you are proud of me again...
tell me, in which universe
is this considered fair?

    i am made of flowers
    i am made of steel
    and for your love, my love,
    my eyes bleed.

AN ETERNAL EARTH

a drop leaves the cloud
and falls on earth as rain
burns by the fire of the sun
but feels no pain
it rises as vapour and
forms the same cloud again.
now, tell me,
when was that drop born?
and when does it die?
does it ever die?
and remind me once again,
what's your body made of?

                i am made of flowers

i am made of steel
and i vow to value my worth,
for i dance on an eternal earth.

FRESH AS FLOWERS

the me in me that is me
never ages
no matter the date on the calendar,
i feel the same way within
as i did when i was in my teens,
and probably, even in my crib...
sure, my form, intelligence and awareness
have evolved with time and life experiences,
but the way i feel inside, knows no age
so thanks dear media and pop-culture
for making me feel less than
by your 'life begins at 30' 'fab at 40'
and '50 and fine' lists...
maybe you mean well
but these things tie up

professional and beauty benchmarks
to our biological age
the truth is,
age is not just a number
age is a myth
the me in me that is me
knows no age
i will never be only 'fab at 40'
i will be broken, scared, sexy,
alive, confused, unsure, confident,
generous, insecure, wholesome...
basically 'everything at 40'..
just like i was 'everything at 20'...
steel never gets old,
it just comes with
a certain manufacturing date
and a flower never gets old too
it is just fresh... or not.
and that's what i am
and always promise to be,
irrespective of the date i came to be,
strong as steel and fresh as flowers...
in full bloom.

>   for i am made of flowers
>   i am made of steel.

ROBBED

i was a child of five
and my cousin was older
when he told me
he found a tape
tucked under his dad's gym bag
he watched it and
made me watch it with him
while i cringed all the way...
that wasn't enough for him
he wanted to see
if that's how it really works.
he told me there was no one else
besides, i had already seen the tape
it could be our little game.
i told him i didn't want to play

but he made me anyway...
...
and that's why i was a child
only till i was five.

>i am made of flowers
>i am made of steel
>and it takes immense courage
>but i am determined to heal.

THE SUN AND THE STARS

time is not ticking away
your watch is
the timepieces are all physical
and you are eternal
so why the mad rush?
the time, the real one,
is always now.
this moment is your eternity.
don't you know you are always there
where you are meant to be?
at times, you may not get to choose
where you are,
but you always get to choose
how you are...
how you feel,

how you think,
how you respond,
how long you stay and
how you go,
wherever it is you want to go...
feeling trapped is a valid emotion
but it's not the truth, it's an illusion
the power of the universe
has been burnt into your bones
your breath is the warmth
that powers the sun.
you look so cute
when you look at your problems
 and think of them as big -
like a toddler
gasping at the height of a swing.
you are adorable when you think
you are powerless, a mere mortal,
that's another one of those illusions..
if you were mortal
how have you conjured up
the absolute magic that is your life
...and your world?
if you were mere mortal,
how do you have stars in your eyes?
if you were mere mortal,

how have you continued to bloom
for an eternity?
in time you will know all you are
for now, just know that
you are made of the sun and the stars
...and if that's too much to take
in one full scoop,
at least accept today that

    you are made of flowers
    and you are made of steel too.

BEHIND CLOSED DOORS

i look at you
and can't help but marvel
at how strong you are...
he did what he did
behind the safety of closed doors.
he tried to act tough
in the darkness of his home
while you are out here
in the real world
reaching out for care
from the right sources
getting help and
helping yourself
out of that darkness.
being vulnerable

for your own sake.
you are turning
to the right people for support
and leaving
the wrong ones behind.
i am amazed
at how strong you are
and of course, so much stronger
than your abuser, that's so obvious.
abusers, sick and vile as they are,
they like to prey on the weak ones
and in your case, wow,
did they pick the wrong one!
keep on being strong
you didn't ask for it,
but you can get through this,
that's why
you were made so strong.

        you are made of flowers
          you are made of steel...
    you've gotten through so much already,
        you'll so get through this.

JUST SAYING

now, i am not asking
all women to love women like me...
that's not how our bodies work
i'm just saying,
when i am with my girlfriend,
and we are fooling around,
we get to tell our bodies
when we want to stop.
not bragging, just saying.

> i am made of flowers,
> i am made of steel,
> and i love someone
> as awesome as me.

70

LOVE AT FIRST FLIGHT

we met on the transit terminal
i was starting my holiday
you were finishing yours
i had a flight out in 2 hours
you had a bus to catch in 40 mins
it was an instant soul connection
we were all awkward first,
then all smiles
there were moments
that, turn by turn,
took both our breaths away
those 40 mins ticked away
in the same heartbeat we both skipped
then the clock declared
the moment had arrived

when destinies turn.
we looked long and hard
into each other's eyes
where possible futures
were being written and rewritten...
then you chose the bus.

...

i could've ditched my holiday
and joined you on the same bus,
but i held back as well.

...

maybe we could've had
so much more
but at least we had those 40 mins.

> i am made of flowers
> i am made of steel
> and i believe all love stories,
> get the right happy endings.

NO RUSH

of course i am not
where i want to be... yet.
but if i won't be content with
where i am right now,
i would only be making
my journey forward painful.
and i love me enough
not to do that to myself.

    i am made of flowers
    i am made of steel
and little by little, i am moving forward
    at my own speed.

THE ETERNAL KIND

your eyes lie to you
you look at the sun,
or a lightbulb,
and your eyes tell you
you are seeing light...
that's only the half truth
the full version of it,
the one your eyes hide,
is that you are seeing
the physical form of light
the true, and the eternal light
is the one you see
when you look at your hand,
or look at yourself in the mirror
...again your eyes will deceive you.

they will tell you, you are looking
at something physical
something finite...
go on,
look at your hand right now,
do it really, look at it.
you'll find yourself wondering
surely this is not how light looks...
that's your mind joining in
on the deception...
the truth is
you are exactly how
the true light,
the eternal kind, looks like...
and it patiently waits for you
to be recognised.

>you are made of flowers,
>   you are made of steel,
>...and you are made of light,
>a light that's made to shine.

A WHOLE LOT OF LOVE

you had your reasons,
some pretty good ones,
still i blamed you
and cried foul for so long.
i claimed you left me
with unbearable heartache,
uncontrollable pain,
immeasurable rage...
but,
i was wrong.
...
you didn't leave me
with any of that.
what you really left me with
is a whole lot of love.

the love i had for you,
all of it,
you left it behind with me.
i was silly
for being mad at you...
before you
i didn't have that love
now i do.
now it's mine. all of it.
and i can do with it
as i please.
thanks for not needing it, stranger,
now, i am spending it all on me.

        i am made of flowers
         i am made of steel.

THE SHIELD

before i was taught
what a bad touch is,
a stranger showed it to me
in the park...
those few minutes
stretched for a lifetime and
covered in magnitude
everything that came after...
that stranger
became my plus 1
everywhere i went in my mind...
he was hurt of course,
else how could he so hurt others?
his inner child
was sad and resentful,

that's why he was so vengeful
...
with time and understanding
i have come to let go of him
to leave him behind in that same park
and move on...
i teach kindergarten now
spend my days with kids
the same age i was then...
i find spending time
with their innocence
and their love filled smiles
healing and comforting...
of course, one of the first things
i teach them, and all my lovely kids,
is how to always stay safe.

    i am made of flowers
    i am made of steel
    and i have turned my trauma
    into my students, and my kids' shield.

75

RADIANCE

gosh, girl!
do you have any clue
just how beautiful you look
when you are doing
what you are born to do.
it's like
the light that you are
just strips away
all that you are not,
and comes
crashing through and
out of every single cell of you...
it's one of the brightest things
i have ever seen,
and yet it doesn't hurt nor blind,

it just envelopes me,
and everything in its path,
in a warm, tight, healing hug.

    you are made of flowers,
      you are made of steel,
        and you are gorgeous
when you wear your soul on your sleeve.

COURAGE

if you don't enjoy
the company you keep
when you are by yourself,
how would anyone else?
if you hide behind your scars
how could anyone
discover the beauty they protect?
if you lead only with your thorns
how would anyone caress
your tenderness?
if you never take the chance,
how will you feel unafraid again?

    you are made of flowers

you are made of steel
and even if you hurt again, I promise,
you'll heal just fine.

MOVING IN

you were talking
and i was thinking
this is the last time
i let anyone set me up...
what a disaster, i thought,
with a smile on my face
to feign interest
in whatever
you were on about
that afternoon in the park...
you were trying
to impress me hard
while i was going through
my mental list
of excuses to bail,

looking for
the least damaging one...
that's why, perhaps,
we both didn't notice
that little child on skates
swoop in and
crash right into your leg...
she fell to the ground
bruised and scared,
looking at your leg
she was
immediately apologetic
and in tears too...
you picked her up,
checked on her bruise
and said something to her,
something i never heard,
and i saw her smile next...

...

i crumpled the list
in my head and
tossed it in the bin...
in that one unguarded moment
you showed me your heart,
and in that
same unguarded moment

MADE OF FLOWERS AND STEEL

my soul decided
your heart was exactly where
it wanted to move in next.

>i am made of flowers,
>i am made of steel,
>and i always follow
>wherever my heart leads.

78

A DANCING SOUL

you have a dancing soul
a content soul,
a singing and a merry soul...
and when you feel black and blue,
down and out, mad and sad,
it's not because
your spirit has forgotten its moves...
it's because you have forgotten
to turn on the music.

>you are made of flowers,
>you are made of steel
>and no matter the odds,
>you can be happy indeed.

A HAPPY PUPPY

the more i run after it
the more it loves to
give me a run for it
the more i chase it
the more it plays tag
with me tirelessly
the more i resist
the more it persists
the more i cry and pine for it
the more it makes me weep
...
i finally figured it out,
i cracked the code...
now, whatever it is
that i want,

the more i smile and let go,
and just let it be,
the more it follows me
like a happy puppy…
the more i allow it,
the more easily
it flows to me
like a river to the sea…
and the less
that i try to cling
and hold on to it,
the easier and the longer
it stays with me.

    i am made of flowers
    i am made of steel
    and now just i let go to
    to attract all i need.

STRENGTH OF CHARACTER

~~grow a pair.~~
grow a vag.

> i look like
> i am made of flowers,
> but i am really
> made of steel.
> and you would be wrong
> to underestimate me.

TIMELESS

it may seem like a cliché
but i fall so easily
for the ones
much, much older than me.
that's just where
the cliché ends though
for i don't have a thing
for silver hair, smile lines
or weathered skins.
i fall hard for the old souls...
the souls that have been
on this eternal journey for a while
long enough to learn
to love everyone as one
to appreciate

the beauty of a cool breeze
to see magic in a raindrop
to know the value of giving
a pat on someone's back...
souls old enough to know
the pricelessness of cuddles,
the souls that know
we only meet to say goodbye...
and we only say goodbye
to say hi again for the first time,
in another time, place or state.
that's the kind of old soul i crave.

> i am made of flowers
> i am made of steel
> i look so young because
> i am a timeless soul deep within.

HOME

i don't know
if reincarnation exists,
but i know that
i'm drawn to a culture
from a country
i wasn't born in.
i am not a linguist but
my heart sings in a tongue
that it should find alien...
i feel more connected
to the people
who look so unlike
me and my flesh,
yet i know
we are fashioned

MADE OF FLOWERS AND STEEL

from the same clay.
i have no memories
of any past lives,
but my head rests easy
on these foreign shores.
i love my country of birth
but another name slips out
when someone asks me
where do i come from...
maybe this is the start
of a higher knowing...
the dawn of knowledge
that i don't really
belong anywhere because
i am one with all,
i am from everywhere.

    i'm made of flowers,
    i'm made of steel.
    my passport says what it will,
    but my heart knows where it lives.

83

MY HAPPY PLACE

there's a
happy little place
near my home
i try to visit it
every day at the happy hour
no there are no specials here,
no 1+2 deals
no house blends too...
there are just paws and woofs
lots and lots of them
jumping and running,
chasing and wagging
sniffing and marking shrubs
with their little trickles...
it doesn't look like much,

but it is one of my
most favourite places
in the world.

        i am made of flowers
        i am made of steel
        and i have never seen anything
        like these little paws so sweet.

THE FEARS I FEEL

'you don't want me to be happy!'
you screamed and
slammed the door in my face
all because i pulled you up
for being out, a little too late
i know my child, this is what
you and your friends want to do...
meet with your friends,
get some coffee and cake,
make your tiktoks
and talk about all the cute boys
from your school.
you are far too young for anything else
and i respect you for knowing it.
please understand, my dear,

when you are out so late,
it's not you that i don't trust,
it's the world.
for i was once old enough as you
and i've never told anyone
but i was late coming home one day
not out of choice,
someone added something
to my lemonade...
when i came to,
i didn't know where i was
and a few hours had passed
till date i don't know who it was
and if they did more to me
than just spike my drink...
and let me tell you,
not knowing what happened
has probably hurt more...
doubt used to paint
indescribable and elaborate
scenes of shame and torture
that i may have been subjected to.
internet wasn't so big back then
but cameras still were
and stories of how
girls had gotten themselves

into trouble
were not uncommon...
i spent a few years
being miserable after,
asking myself
if something wrong
even happened...
for a time,
i convinced myself
i must have passed out
because of something bad i ate
but the doubts remained...
'how could i be so stupid?!'
i use to berate myself...
i lost some of my best years
to that doubt and that hurt,
and was left with
a ton of mistrust.
slowly i got brave,
even slower, i learnt to let go
slower still, i learnt to heal...
that was when, i met your father
maybe that's why
love didn't show up till then.
the time i lost, i never got back
and that's why i am

a little too hard on you, my dear
but i know it's not healthy,
so, let's make a deal
now, shall we?
i will learn
to let go more,
to trust you more.
i won't project
my yesterday on your today.
and you, my dear,
you just be
a little more mindful
out there in the world,
and be smarter than
i ever was, or will be,
and, together,
we will make it just fine.

> you are made of flowers
> you are made of steel,
> and my trust on you, my child,
> is greater than the fears i feel.

THE WAR WITHIN

my bones ache
my brain cells scream in agony
my head is heavy on the pillow
my heart weighs a ton
my eyes are weary
my arms and legs are made of lead
my body moves like i am hundred...
all this and more shows up
when i am fighting my spirit and
insisting on doing things my way
...
when i let go and
let the flow direct my way,
my step is lighter
my heart feels softer

MADE OF FLOWERS AND STEEL

i have the energy of a teen
and magic shows up in my life
like it is the new normal...
moment by moment,
i am way happier.

        i am made of flowers
        i am made of steel
    and in this tango-waltz of life
    i am letting the universe lead.

WORK IN PROGRESS

if you are here
it's not too late.

    you are made of flowers
    you are made of steel
    and the story
    of your spectacular comeback
    is still incomplete.

THE SILENT WITNESS

i am standing in the rain.
it's pouring,
coming down
heavy and hard.
if i make it real
it can give me
a nasty cold
drench and drown me even...
if i detach from it and
just see myself
standing there,
i can see the beauty of it
because if i can
see myself in the rain
then i am not the one

standing in the rain
the eye cannot see itself
without a mirror.
so if i can see myself
standing there with
my awareness
then i am not the one
standing there getting wet,
i am the one
looking at a mirror image,
i am the one who is watching.
so how could
that rain hurt me
if i am not even there?
as i come to know
the fact that i am safe,
i choose to
dance in that rain
to let it wash over me
to cleanse me, to purify me...
...
the rain is my emotions,
the one standing there
is what i think i am,
the one observing
this wonderful dance

is the consciousness
that i really am.
as are you.

>i am made of flowers
>i am made of steel
>and i surprise myself
>when i go so deep.

UNIQUENESS

the creator,
whoever you
believe it to be,
gave you a completely
unique fingerprint
dna unique enough
to stand strong as evidence
retina different enough
to unlock government vaults
voice distinct enough
that even siri
can recognise it in billions…
and with all this
precious uniqueness
how dare you blend in

and fade into the background?
you are made to stand out
you are made to shine
your voice is meant to be heard
your story is meant to be told
your life is to become a legend
you are meant to do, be and have
everything you can imagine
doing, being and having.

> for you are made of flowers
> you are made of steel
> and for a mighty good reason,
> you are made so unique.

YOUR BLANK PAGE

you have
a secret to keep?
trust me with it
i'll hide it
in the best place on earth,
right in front of everyone.
your shoulders are drooping,
you've been stooping,
you've been
lugging it everywhere...
you are tired
you are scared
you are ashamed
don't you see,
you are the one

who's clutching it
but
you are also the one
getting crushed?
let it go now.
let it all out,
let me be your voice,
let me be your stage,
let me be your blank page...
it's not as bad as
you think it is
and once you put it down
you'll wonder, you'll see,
what was the big deal...
it only hurts
when you hold on.
just spell it out
it doesn't have to be hard,
i won't judge
we are all allowed
a few mistakes after all...
that's how this
being 'human' thing works
now that you know better,
you'll do better next time.
for the new song to begin

the old one must end,
so be done with the past
it's where the ghosts live...
you live here today
and it is such a perfect place
for the new to begin.

    you are made of flowers,
      you are made of steel
  and i am here, dear stranger,
      to help you heal.

EVER AFTER

i'm still waiting
for someone to ask my soul
out on a date
their soul and mine
will go for a walk by the lake
one will bring a mat
the other, their pet cat
one will bring a guitar
the other, a guide to the stars
talk will be optional
the vibe unconditional
we'll swim in each other's eyes
feast on shared dreams
and get drunk
on our laughter...

we'll spend an eternity,
and a happily ever after,
all in that single day,
the day our souls
go out on a date.

    i am made of flowers,
    i am made of steel
and our souls, my love,
    are meant to meet.

WE GOT THIS

i find it mighty amusing
how the world feels compelled
to tell a woman how she should live…
rest easy, dear world
we've been doing this for a while…
and we are crushing it.

> we look like we are made of flowers
> but we are really made of steel.

92

TAGS

she
he
him her
binary
non-binary
we can discuss
demand and debate
about pronouns
all we want
but i feel,
the only pronouns
that truly matter are
we and us.

MADE OF FLOWERS AND STEEL

we are made of flowers,
we are made of steel
and underneath all our different labels,
we share the same heartbeat.

CONTENT

i am
born of this earth
i belong to
a shared universe
knowing this,
i aim to cause no harm...
to anyone, in any way.
i realise i may fail at times
i am only human.
so i am quick to apologise
and fast to forgive.
if i fail at everything else
but succeed at this one goal,
to cause no harm, to tread lightly
and lovingly on this earth,

i will call it a good life,
i will be content.

    i am made of flowers
    i am made of steel
    i have grand ambitions
    and being human tops the list.

SEEN AND HEARD

hey,
how are you?
no, i won't accept
a well-rehearsed and
a canned response.
tell me really,
be honest now,
how are you really?
if no one is around
say it out loud
shout it out
if you like...
if there are people around
write it on a piece of paper
or as a text on your phone

do it.
you don't have to send that text
or show that note to anyone
but you need to voice
and listen
to your thoughts
and your emotions.
just tell me now,
tell me please.
i won't be able
to hear your words
but trust me,
you will be heard.
go on, tell me
how are you really?

>   you are made of flowers,
>   you are made of steel
>   and the more you voice your feelings,
>   the better you will feel.

GUARDED

my walls are up
not to keep you out,
but to keep me safe.
and that's your clue,
if you want my walls
to come down,
all you gotta do
is to make me
feel safe with you.
will it be
a bit of work?
you bet.
will it be worth it?
that's for me to know
and for you to find out.

MADE OF FLOWERS AND STEEL

i am made of flowers
i am made of steel
and i'll give you a hint,
'how valuable are the things
you keep under lock and key?'

A CHANCE ENCOUNTER

nearly 8 billion
on the planet
so how come we meet
only the people we meet?
it cannot be sheer co-incidence
for then it will be
far too many co-incidences
for any logical person
to believe them.
so i choose to believe
we meet for a very specific purpose
we meet to learn from each other
we meet to love each other
we meet to heal each other
for all of us are

hurting somewhere inside
there's something we desire
that has been alluding us far too long
there's something in us
that's restless, that's tired, that's scared
something that craves to be acknowledged
something that needs encouragement
a seed deep inside that will thrive
when nourished with a kind word
...
i believe our paths cross
to have these needs met.
our paths cross
so that we can help each other
on our journey home...
to a place where
we will still be us, only higher.
and if we help each other,
here, today,
we will get there faster, together.
that's why, out of 8 billion
permutations and combinations,
only our paths have crossed
for these few fleeting moments.
that's why,
i am learning to remind myself

whenever i meet someone,
to go within and ask myself,
how can i help this person?
when we help
enough people find home,
we will find ourselves home.
that's what this journey is all about.

>
> we are made of flowers
> we are made of steel
> and there's a good reason why
> we meet the ones we meet.

CONQUER

so what if you
weren't born a princess?
fasten your armour,
draw your sword,
channel your inner warrior,
find somewhere sunny,
and win yourself
a nice little *'kingdom'*
princess is good.
warrior queen is better.

    you are made of flowers
    you are made of steel
    and you are strong enough
    to create the life you want to lead.

THE DEAL

i am a woman
and i have fixed a leak
beneath the kitchen sink,
changed the fuse
when it was shot,
replaced a flat tyre
on the way back
with the kids
from the park,
all these things
i wasn't born
knowing how to do...
i learnt some of them online,
some i taught myself to do...
so if you want to be

the man in my life
the excuse of
'honey, i would love
to help out in the kitchen
but i don't know how...'
just won't do.
if i can learn, why can't you?

    i am made of flowers
    i am made of steel
    and we can be happy together
    if 'we are in this together,' is the deal.

FAMILY

i started out
as a drunken mistake.
my mom, a raging alcoholic,
didn't want me,
and my dad was too busy
to get to know me.
child services
tried to protect me
the best way they could,
their intentions were good.
i ended up being tossed
family to family
moving towns, schools,
losing friends before they were close.
by the time i was an adult,

MADE OF FLOWERS AND STEEL

i had lived with numerous families
but not a single one i could call my own.
then i decided to end
the little pity party in my head
i got 2 jobs while at my uni
and i got my first pet...
that was 7 years ago
now here we are
and it seems i live in a zoo!
i have 2 dogs, 2 parrots, a parakeet,
a tortoise, 4 gold fish,
a cat with a new litter, and
a beehive with who knows how many bees.
somewhere playing among them,
there is a boyfriend too...
all families are different,
and i love how adorable mine is.

> i am made of flowers
> i am made of steel
> and i love the family
> i built for me.

TINPOT

tinpot.
the name i started calling you
when you were four...
at home, and in private, of course
it was our little secret
you would hate me for it
but i would silence your objections with
'i made you, i can call you what i like'
and you would roll your big eyes...
around 7 yrs, wasn't it,
you would smile a broken smile
lined with windows
traded for the tooth fairy's silver coin
how we played together when you were nine
how i longed to see you for the first time

the nine months
couldn't have passed any slower...
and they never did.
...
it was only 4 months
you spent with me, within me...
i never even got to see you...
so how do i so miss the moments
i never got to live with you?

    i am made of flowers
    i am made of steel
but without you, my sweet little tinpot,
    i will always be incomplete.

*

Now, I must leave your hand, let you free in the world to find your own adventures. I hope these pages have provided comfort and helped you get in touch with the steel in you. The world can be a hard place at times, but I believe you'll do just fine. You have everything you need, and everywhere you go, you bring the beauty within. It only gets better from here on.

— LOVE, SAMEER KOCHURE.

*

Do you believe this book can help more women out there? If you answered yes, kindly leave a review and talk about this book on your social feeds. It will take you a few minutes, but it just may help a sister in some corner of the world rediscover her steel. For that, just like me, she'll be forever grateful to you.

I have written about my influences and how I wrote this book in the acknowledgment section, so check it out if you like.

Before that, here's a sneak peek at another book series of mine that you may enjoy as well.

A YOUNG BOY
and his best friend,
THE UNIVERSE

Welcome to a spiritual fable that will win your heart.

SEE the world through the eyes of a young boy that are full of wonder and innocence.

The young boy sees what others don't and questions what the grownups won't. And boy, does he have questions. A pocket full of them.

Luckily for him, he has an equally playful friend, the Universe, by his side. The Universe helps him make sense of the world. The young boy's best friend, the Universe knows everything and helps him through life's mysteries, like a true friend.

Fall in love with these two unique characters as they laugh, cry and play together.

Discover a friendship that will leave you longing

for a similar friendship in your own life. And don't be too surprised if you find yourself in the young boy's shoes once too often.

That's when you'll be the closest to your new best friend.

Part of Sameer Kochure's 'The Good Universe Series' - these books can be read and enjoyed in any order.

Turn the page to read excerpt from this much loved series now.

AN UNIMPORTANT THING

"Money is not important, right?" the young boy asked.

"Absolutely," the Universe replied lazily. "That's why make a lot of it. After all, which wise man or smart woman would like to spend his or her precious time, and mind, worrying about an unimportant thing like money... or the lack of it?"

The young boy nodded, rolled up his Spiderweb-Man shirt sleeves and went to work.

The Universe got its chequebook out.

That was the 1st Chapter from Vol. I. ⇧
Buy Now.

BIG PLANS

"Good morning!" the young boy said.

"Good mo...rrrning..." the Universe replied yawning.

"So, what shall we do today?" the young boy asked.

"Let's laugh today."

And they did.

It was a great day.

∾

That was Chapter 1 from Vol. II. ⇧
 Buy Now.

A CLOUDY DAY

THE YOUNG BOY SAID, "Sometimes I feel there is no point to it all. I just want to end everything... for good."

The skies were dark.

"Hmm... tell me, have you ever received a gift that was shabbily packed?" the Universe asked.

"Yeah... on my last birthday."

"Well, life is like that. Sometimes on the surface, it may feel like you have been handed a pretty

lousy one. But it is a gift, nonetheless. Look beyond the appearances, and you'll discover treasure inside.

It may take some time for you to realise just how precious it is. But would you ever throw away

a present without even opening it, just because it looks shabby?"

'Never! What if there are rollerblades inside and

the one who got it for me didn't have the time to wrap it nicely and had to rush to the party?" the young boy replied.

"Exactly. Same is with life. Maybe the one who wrapped it up for you was also running late. Maybe he spent so much time looking for a priceless one for you, that there was no time left for fancy packaging."

"Hmm..," the young boy thought about it for a while.

The Universe asked gently, "It's better to allow the time for the gift to reveal itself, right?"

"Yeah! Maybe there are rollerblades AND a spaceship inside!!" the young boy's eyes lit up.

The clouds thundered, and the rain came crashing down.

"Paper boats time?" the Universe suggested.

The young boy smiled and started looking for an old newspaper.

You just read Chapter 6 from Vol. III. ⇧
Buy Now.

ALL RIGHT

"How many people can be right in an argument?" said the young boy.

"All of them. But none of them are."

"How come?"

The Universe said, "Because they are arguing."

The young boy went quiet. Then he nodded, smiling.

His heart was bigger than his ego.

The Universe beamed happiness at him.

That was Chapter 6 from Vol. VII. ⇧
Buy Now.

ACKNOWLEDGMENTS

Seven months ago, I set myself an impossible task. To write a poetry book about women.

As a man writing about women, I expect I have got a lot of things wrong about how women think and feel. The blame for that lies with me.

The credit for what I got right goes to at least a million women out there who helped me write this book. Before we discuss their contribution, let me take you right to the beginning.

I give thanks to my mom and dad, Sunanda Pramod Kochure and Pramod Kochure, where my story began.

My dear sister and brother-in-law, Dr Monica and Dr Narahari, and my nephew Hriday, who are true warriors and conquerors. They always have a song and smiles to share with everyone.

Last year I saw my sister take on a challenge at work and overcome it with absolute dedication and unwavering commitment. Her strength of character inspired me to write a poem for her that became her birthday gift, and the seed from which this book flowered.

So, I owe her gratitude, and if you enjoyed this book, you do too.

Next, my extended family, my dear aunt Viju maushi, Tayade uncle, Gauri, Pinks, Sam, Ishaan, Khrisha and family. They make me feel connected and grounded.

While the Creator, my parents and my family have given me this life, my spiritual teachers are teaching me how to live it.

I am so blessed that the list of the ones I consider my spirit guides keeps getting longer every single day.

I offer my reverential and deepest gratitude to José Silva, Dr Bimol Rakshit, Ding Le Mei, Gautama Buddha, SN Goenka, Mandeep Kaur madam, Vinay Rathod sir, Hemil Shah sir, Tejal Mamaniya, and many more. To all of you, I give thanks, I give thanks.

Now we come back to the million women whose stories inspired these poems.

Writing one poem for my sister was easy, because I had seen her in action closely. But I knew if I had to write a book celebrating the mettle in women, it had to be rooted in truth. I couldn't just make it up, it wouldn't be right.

So, with this, my sixth book, for the first time, I turned to research. I joined female centric online groups and forums. I dived deeper into lives of female influencers, vloggers, musicians, authors and entrepreneurs. I researched TED talks, interviews, studies on gender gap, rising demand for cosmetic surgery, porn addiction in women, challenges conceiving, and practically anything I could get my hands on.

I was always looking for the answer to a single question - how do women overcome the challenges they face?

Being a silent observer on these open-for-all forums gave me an insider's view of how women take on their life problems. It was one of the most heartbreaking and inspiring things I have ever seen. Tears were shared and victories celebrated.

The sheer volume and variety of problems women face for simply being women is staggering. The only way they can rise above them, and they do so graciously, is with absolute grit.

Their problems and strength have inspired each and every poem in this collection.

To protect individual identities and out of respect, I have taken creative license and fictionalised 90% of the content, but the resilience at the heart of every poem, is 100% rooted in reality.

It's my way of honouring the real women fighting real battles every day.

This book is also dedicated to you, dear reader. To the feminine energy, the flowers and steel in you. It's my way of cheering you on and wishing you victory.

You deserve it.

Lastly, I am just the voice, the pen that moves on command. The words and the wisdom that move you come from the all loving Universe.

For that, and so much more, I give thanks, dear Universe. Keep using me as you will.

Love,

Sameer Kochure.

19th July 2021.

Wrong. An Inspirational Poetry Collection

Get a FREE copy of Sameer Kochure's new book at: www.ChannelingHigherWisdom.com

About the Book:

NASA's Voyager 1 has captured a strange, rhythmic, humming sound vibrating in interstellar space.

Could it be the Universe speaking to us in poetry?

Thus begins this powerful inspirational poetry collection by Sameer Kochure, author of the much adored book series 'A Young Boy And His Best Friend, The Universe.'

Just like that beloved spiritual fable, *this book is full of wisdom shorts that'll help you live a more wholesome life*.

It takes *the inner eye, a thinking heart and a feeling mind,* to appreciate all the beauty that surrounds us. There's just so much of it out there, and the loving Universe that it is; it feeds it to us in small, right-sized portions, the ones we can truly love and appreciate.

No wonder, we keep coming back for more.

Get it FREE at
www.ChannelingHigherWisdom.com

ALSO BY SAMEER KOCHURE

The Good Universe Series:

A Young Boy and His Best Friend, The Universe Vol. I

A Young Boy and His Best Friend, The Universe, Vol. II

A Young Boy and His Best Friend, The Universe, Vol. III

A Young Boy and His Best Friend, The Universe, Vol. VII

A Young Boy and His Best Friend, The Universe. Boxset: Books 1-3

The 1 Verse Poetry Collection:

Made of Flowers and Steel

Wrong - An Inspirational Poetry Collection

www.ChannelingHigherWisdom.com

YOUR SHORT STORY

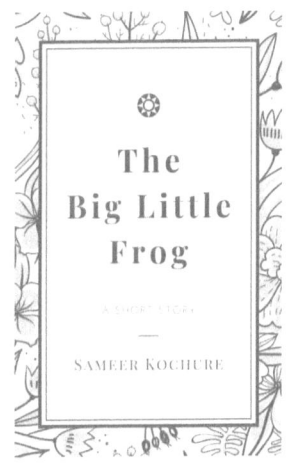

Get a free short story - **The Big Little Frog** as a welcome hug for signing up for my newsletter. The story is a powerful allegory about the consequences of our choices. It's a short read with a big payoff, told with lyrical charm. You'll enjoy it.

Read it at: www.ChannelingHigherWisdom.com

ABOUT THE AUTHOR

Author photo by Ahsan Ali

Sameer Kochure was born in India during the darkest part of the night. Probably explains why he is such a self-proclaimed dreamer. He has lived in 6 cities and 3 countries since. He has also clocked in 12 years as a Creative Director in some of the biggest advertising agencies across Asia Pacific. He lives in

Dubai, but claims that anywhere he travels, he feels he is home.

You can follow Sameer on the following social channels and join his VIP mailing list at:
www.ChannelingHigherWisdom.com

CARE SECTION

Here is some information I hope and pray you never need. Below you'll find a list of a few helpful resources. It'll save you a search if that's not an option. Kindly do due diligence before reaching out to them. This is by no means a full and comprehensive list, better organisations may be available near you. I just wanted to give you an idea that no matter how daunting the challenges you may be facing, you don't have to face them alone. Help is available. Reach out. Get the help you need. Stay strong.

If you are someone who has experienced sexual harassment or assault and wish to speak with a trained professional about it, these hotlines and organisations can listen to your experiences and make referrals to counsellors and support groups to the extent of your comfort.

Global Resources

RAINN: https://www.rainn.org/ 24/7 Crisis support for victims/survivors of sexual assault. Over the phone or through instant messaging. If your country is not listed below, you can contact RAINN to be referred to a local organisation.

US:

Crisis Text Line https://www.crisistextline.org/ You can text 741-741 24/7 from any cell phone in the United States to be anonymously connected to a trained crisis counsellor. They also have anonymous Facebook messenger and Kik options if you do not have access to a cell phone.

One in Six http://1in6.org An organisation for male-identified survivors of sexual assault. Provides anonymous individual and group counselling 24/7 through online chat functions

CARE SECTION

National Domestic Violence Hotline http://www.thehotline.org Provides 24/7 anonymous crisis and counselling support over the phone, and anonymous online chat crisis and counselling support from 7am until 2am Central Time

Anti-Violence Project https://avp.org/ Provides 24/7 anonymous phone based crisis and counselling for LGBTQ identified victims of assault and violence, including sexual assault and violence. Based in New York but can refer nationwide

DoD Safe Helpline https://www.safehelpline.org/ Provides 24/7 phone and online chat based crisis and counselling for victims of sexual assault and harassment serving in the military, or who are employed by the Department of Defence.

US Volunteer network providing emotional support and care to women who need abortions or body autonomy. https://www.reddit.com/r/auntienetwork/
https://www.facebook.com/groups/844874665870462/

Canada

CARE SECTION

Canada's crisis hotlines are organised by province and subject matter, [here](http://www.dawncanada.net/issues/issues/we-can-tell-and-we-will-tell-2/crisis-hotlines/) is a comprehensive list of hotlines and organisations.

UK

Rape Crisis England & Wales https://rapecrisis.org.uk/ Provides online resources 24/7 and live support over the phone in the afternoons and evenings.

SupportLine http://www.supportline.org.uk/ Provides online resources 24/7 and live support over the phone during the day and evening.

Additional Resources from BBC UK https://www.bbc.co.uk/programmes/articles/22VVM5LPrf3pjYdKqctmMXn/information-and-support-sexual-abuse-and-violence

Europe

CARE SECTION

Rape Crisis Network Europe https://www.rcne.com/ Provides online resources and live support for anyone living in Europe

Australia

1800respect https://www.1800respect.org.au and their phone number, 1800 737 732.

Kids Helpline https://www.www.kidshelpline.com.au for people under 25 also 1800 55 1800

International Suicide Prevention Wiki Covers information for many countries, thanks to the powerful postsecret.com project

https://suicideprevention.wikia.org/wiki/International_Suicide_Prevention_Directory

BUY OR BORROW

Libraries played a big part in nurturing my love for reading while growing up. So to give back some of the love libraries have shown me, I have made sure that all my books are easily accessible to major libraries across the world. In case, you don't find any of my books that you want at your library, just fill out a simple book request form, all libraries have them, and more often than not, they will be happy to procure my books for you and honour your request. They love supporting loyal readers like you. Libraries are awesome that way. Show them some love as well. :)

GRATITUDE

Thank you for reading.

May your flowers always bloom, and your steel always shimmer in your light.

www.ingramcontent.com/pod-product-compliance
Lightning Source LLC
LaVergne TN
LVHW041917070526
838199LV00051BA/2642